Shelley Cinema and other poems

Shelley Cinema

and other poems

Stephen Gray

PROTEA BOOK HOUSE
PRETORIA
2006

Shelley Cinema and other poems – Stephen Gray

First edition, first impression 2006

Protea Book House
PO Box 35110, Menlopark, 0102
1067 Burnett Street, Hatfield, 0083
protea@intekom.co.za

Typography and design by Tiglix Digital Communication
Cover page by Tiglix Digital Communication
Printed and bound by Paarl Print

ISBN 1-86919-095-5
© 2006 Stephen Gray
© All rights reserved. No part of this book may be reproduced
without the permission of the publisher.

Contents

Introduction   7

*   *   *

David at Settlers Bar   13
Rashid the Voyager   14
Hank the Aids-Warrior   15
Reinaldo of the Bistro   17
Yassine the Moor   18
Marcus from Maseru   19
Paulus his Brother   20
Bernhard the Peace-Monitor   21
José the Counter-Tenor   23
Stanley Kiss-and-Tell   24
Hansie the TV   25
Prince the Flower-Seller   26
Millennium Burn-Artist   28
Henno the Diver   30
I. and J. Leave for the Big Apple   32
MY NAME IS JAMIE   34
Nuru the Peddler's Christmas   36

*   *   *

Alternative Route   41
Singing Dunes   42
Hoopoe   43
The Black Eagles of Roodekrans   44
Lake Asal   46

*   *   *

Room Service   49
Body Language   50
Proposal   53

*   *   *

Mad Poet in His Tower   57
On a Lock of Pushkin's Hair   59
On the Body of Ché Guevara   60
On Hannibal, General   61
An African Elegy   62
On the Grave of Sarah Baartman   63

*   *   *

Chain Letter   67
Hippo   68
Learning Italian   69
On Those Learned Quills   70
Translating Montale   71

*   *   *

Shelley Cinema   77

*   *   *

64 Short poems   93

*   *   *

The Leper Band   111

Introduction

Feeling that I should explain myself, being a South African abroad, on 5 March, 1996, I began as follows:

When recently I came to write my autobiography, I kept turning up factors which I began to call the accident of my birth. There are three essential circumstances about oneself that one can do nothing about: *when* one is born (in 1941, so I am perforce now middle middle aged); *where* (in Cape Town so, like three quarters of the world's population at that time, I was a being colonised by Europe, in my case by England and its language, in a country that no longer exists – the Union of South Africa); and *who* – my lineage was Scottish-Irish, middle-class Protestant white, of the usual settler stock which for several generations had been South African passport-holders.

None of that could I do much *about*. But the challenge of my life as I have come to see it was to do something *with* it: not to be imprisoned in the circumstances of that accident, but to make the best of it – to find something that was mine to devote myself to, in a way that was honourable and also offered a half-way decent livelihood.

As everyone surely must now know, the situation was not uncomplicated. South Africa was doomed to go into the apartheid period, which lasted from 1948 and was really beginning to show itself for what it was with the Sharpeville Massacre of 1960. Unlike the vast majority of South Africans at the time, I was privileged to have some options. As I was not brought up to be especially brave, at first I chose to turn my back on it all – in my late teens and early twenties I wandered the world, trying to become a citizen of anywhere but South Africa.

I had a good crack at becoming a North American hippie and flower-child, at a fine time in your culture when we deluded ourselves into believing that it was indeed possible for like-minded people here to build an alternative lifestyle to that of your status quo. In a way I still belong to that other world, which I am utterly dismayed no longer to find a trace of. But yet, if I'd had just a little more elbow-room, I would probably have stayed on, becoming an American I guess, although in my heart – and for a poet more important, on my tongue – never truly having the words to belong.

So it came time to plod back to and confront my heritage. Within hours of my return to South Africa in 1969 I knew I had been fated to make the right decision: the words came. And they kept on coming. Many South African writers who were permitted to stay within the country suffered state control – not to put too fine a point on it: censorship, in some cases the bullet – and all of us have had our world distorted, pulled out of true. Clearing and maintaining a sane and safe context, then, is our beholden duty.

In South Africa one is also the inheritor of a tough-minded school of work: Olive Schreiner, whose *The Story of an African Farm* of 1883 began the Empire writing back to the motherland strain; Alan Paton, whose *Cry, the Beloved Country* was first published by Scribner in 1948; Es'kia Mphahlele, Nadine Gordimer, Athol Fugard and so on. They have all managed to be relatively uncompromised, while producing work of utmost integrity. It has been my job to follow on there.

As you must also know, South Africans found themselves redeemed two years ago when through democratic elections the new government of the ANC came to power, with the quite extraordinary Nelson Mandela as our State President. Not too many of us thought there would be such a joyful outcome in our history, with so little bloodshed, nor that that forlorn African country would ever have a hope in hell of a second chance.

So now I am situated where an alternative world is being built in the last place on earth where it was foreseeable, and all the luckier to be part of that. And we have room for strugglistas, too, who may be searching for a winning cause.

That is how I am positioned, and I thank you for your hospitality.

This speech was first given at the Harry Ransom Humanities Research Center at the University of Texas at Austin, where incidentally my collection of papers has since come to rest. There I began a poetry-reading tour of the United States which led me to Bloomington, Stony Brook, Amherst, Harvard... explaining my first country, and my position as a poet within it, all the way through what I realised was at heart my strange second country.

My third country, it turns out, has become Italy. There on 6 September, 2001, at the Mantua Festival of Literature I was invited to perform before a bilingual audience my "Translating Montale", the poem written for precisely such an occasion. My previous slim volume of 1998 (*Gabriel's Exhibition*, published by Mayibuye Books), had partly been written in Italy in the previous few years. After the Mantua event I made a pilgrimage to the Bay of Poets, arriving at Lerici, off which Shelley was drowned, by 11 September.

Now I was accumulating another collection of items in which the Italian element would be as evident as the American, but which as yet lacked an organising principle. Then I found Giovanni Paolo Pannini's composite painting called "Picture Gallery with Views of Modern Rome" (actually in the Museum of Fine Arts, Boston), one of a hundred such anthologising works of the eighteenth century. It is a single oil painting, containing arrangements of many oil paintings by subject.

So here enter the antechamber, which houses the portraits. Then we come upon the landscapes with nature studies. The passage is lined with the courtship theme, before the main display of history pieces. Another colonnade in our shrinking perspective leads off to the Italian room, where matters of translation are depicted.

And then, because this is the early twenty-first century, given over more to the media than traditional means of expression, your ticket entitles you to enter the darkened Shelley Cinema, back left. There a homage to the Romantic Movement and the Silent Screen is currently showing.

Back right is just the workroom where my cartoons of the last decade are tacked up on pinboards, about the exit to the world outside.

Grateful acknowledgements are due to first publishers: to John Kinsella for "Translating Montale" (in *Stand*, Leeds, September, 1999); to Shirley Chew for "Shelley Cinema" (in *Moving Worlds*, Leeds, Vol. 2, No. 2, 2002); and to Ian Ayres for "Hank the Aids-Warrior" (in *Van Gogh's Ear*, The French Connection Press, Paris, 2004).

Stephen Gray
Johannesburg, 2006

* * *

David at Settlers Bar

David, in the Settlers Bar: strictly Carling and Stuyvesant,
but there were times when bottles of brandy, only dagga did.

So you're twice the man, ox-solid now, a real hunk,
no longer cringing for crime – chest-expanding as you talk

and talk away; has long-distance talk become your profession?
Barfly chatter, flex the elbow, exhale, being unfaithful

to your delicate, newborn lover? (We blah about the dogs
they cherish – Dora the dachsie and Bess the corgi and Bertolt:

like me of no particular breed, but *so* handsome, so deeply butch…)
Still he binges (lover lets slip), weekends till he's knocked out

in the Coloured location: grows invincible, snaps people's valuables,
has to take peace jobs in gardens, go back on the trail, apologise, pay up.

But still he *knew* me the moment I ventured in for what, a A – Amstel?:
up in Joburg… Mayfair, that old house… yes, nineteen-ninety,

ninety-one… used to take him back, barely satisfied,
to his tolerant folks, three o'clock, given a lif'

to Eldorado Park… oh David, hardly the bashful stutterer you grew out of,
not yet yourself: found a world of your own (plural) to move into.

Yes, *true-love* now, with his la-di-da, daft teacher of goodwill…
settled, with those hounds. Wha'd you say your name was again? Cheers.

Rashid the Voyager

Met passing notes – at another conference where everyone had to lie,
theoretical lies, political lies, cheating lies – moved knee to knee.

Isn't Foucault dead yet? – After the election there'll be no more of this
academic kak for sure!! *All Engels full Marx?* And I'm a vegetarian, too.

Your nametag? *My name is R-A-S-H-I-D.* How do you do? Let's slip out...
In the sauna he confessed he was half-Pope, half-Shiva, and I admitted:

He could see neither for me, but what about a bit of the other? That too.
But then smiling – always smiling, Rashid – was voted upwardly

mobile young black scholar, learning fast also to lie through his teeth.
Postcards from Brazil, San Francisco, Delhi: I won't forget you...

and then daringly, a stick-on heart... and two of those overlapping, red.
Playing straight on the circuit, sleeping not with any Great Master,

but with their second-hand wives... Research is never finding
    what you know already
(my darling), nor should new intellectuals be paid to state old truths.

GAVE MY PAPER ON BAD APARTHEID SEXUALITY / TOURED
THE STATES TRIUMPHANT TO NEW YORK / REMAINING CHASED FOR YOU,

OR IS THAT CHASTE? (in Honolulu)... And so, with all that
High-Flying, Rashid had amassed his tithe of Voyager miles.

Equal now. He'd not lose that bonus excursion to Johannesburg,
where at last we would meet and evade no longer, use lip and tongue

to spell out a fresh agenda (as they say), hands to discover
the one out there other than ourself, travel closer. Stop lying.

Hank the Aids-Warrior

Burned off his youth getting rid of the bad government,
now taking care for us all of the next one's AIDS policy:

bandies the jargon: retro-, pro-tease, inhibits, AZT,
piggybacks on STDs, from a migrant father into your hapless ma;

will-less your captains of industry, community leaders, Ministers of Health
do not – have AIDS; because of them everyone else – has AIDS:

cliometrics: in ten years 6 million of ours, piled up, no place to bury...
this means, when you park your car, if you still have a car
     and somewhere to go,

so many more orphans, hundreds of thousands, offering themselves for bread:
old Hanky-Pank, has to prophesy the new apocalypse and Save

the Nation. Cause we all screw around too much (speak for yourself),
promiscuous and unprotected; it's the chief-choses-virgin

at the snake-dance ritual, leather boss picks apprentice
at the railway hostel more likely, that drive to Risk the Reaper:

none of your European namby-pamby quick-come in a plastic bag, no hell:
flesh to flesh, mucous to membrane, it's A-fri-ca...
     long blood-time, spit-time!

In Harare, Gaborone, coffins on the roadside are cheaper for those
dying slim... it's *our* rates now, the worst in the whole world...

thanks to such frittering away. My dear, what about you yourself,
Hanky-Panky-Spank, proving there's hysteria in hardy campaigners,

with your lube and your chains and Saturday night donors, *safe
my broer* and taking the tip... leaving messages after the beep

that never comes. The doom scenario you get off on now,
your marked, shiftless citizens no longer engaged in love,
   but in their dying cause.

Reinaldo of the Bistro

Big-eyed. Who used to cook for us at the Bistro, where always
his specials really were. Took my foreign researchers

for an authentic ostrich steak or wait for it – once kudu
pizzaiola. Just his vegetable soup fuelled wan legions...

Slurry his speech, but we considered that held -s his lazy-bones
way of greeting (ex-alcoholic?), fiddling his crucifix from his chest hair,

saving his cigarette for the extractor: so welcoming, but a bit blue.
A storm of cooking up, then the mild, big-eyed way when he personally served.

Spelt dyslexically: once we had BELGAIN WAFFLES... chalked
up on the pavement black-board, soaked in cream and NATALE HONEY.

Turns out your life-companion, your neatest front-man, is now
    in unbuttoned despair
as from the depths of mourning emerge a lost mother, a hard wife too,

your legal dependents never known to have taken care of you:
    want your jewels,
want *his* insurance... Poor Reinaldo, who hated medicine, used food instead.

What can I make for you now, gentlemen? See, I have a nice
little, juicy little, not too stringy, not stringy at all, in fact:

tumour, like a nail through his brain, diagnosed and paralysed
within the first day; after flailing, on the second day dead.

Didn't have AIDS, hepatitis or malaria or even TB, just a normal
way out. And I have a lovely fresh, not too creamy, but tart,

a bit bitter, well it's like a s-sorbet, just to rinse-se
the palate of my regular banqueters, just for you, dears: no extra charge.

Yassine the Moor

With Othello as pedigree, from the University of Casablanca,
older than Europe's – such a promising c. v. (no bursaries, jobs):

across all the new Africa on Air Maroc (no permanent visa),
working in passage, waiting for tips, learning this another language.

How do you say zootcase, djeans, trainers, T-shirt, bracelet,
all stolen at Backpackers in Randburg, no declaration to any police.

In all his illegal years I'd fetch him from White Land to mosque,
where at least in Arabic respite he dreamed on: at sunset, break fast...

Never laid hand on him: his weightlifter's chest and blue chin,
hourglass waist and raiding knuckles... Once at my knees (we'd been

swimming privately all afternoon, off duty, affectionate),
    he pinched his flesh
harshly: *Never I'll succeed, see I'm too dark for your people...*

(he had married one of us by then, and I was their best man;
not the besotted girl he needed, but a permit to stay out of Home Affairs,

abandoned her – it was convenience)... *Here I am just an alien still,
I should be your slave! Cut my head off and put on a pole!*

We had disturbed a swallow's nest under the diving-board,
and now even huge Yassine the Blackamoor, panicked and wild-eyed,
    was divebombed

by her. *You see, even the birds in your country!* Before she struck
him – mid-forehead – parting his curly hair. Back for attack! Evacuate!

Ah Yassine, as migrant as that little soul, in the end. Never laid
a hand on, but his God did. Seeking his fortune further. Blessed.

Marcus from Maseru

His knees about me like earmuffs. Said this was only – what? –
good manners. I said don't feel you must oblige. Your room

is your room as long as you're my guest, and mine stays mine.
    Gets chilly, brr, lonely:
lumbers about in a blanket and slip for yet another beer.

Does press-ups with much display of snort and grunt on the wooden floor.
Come to the Big City by taxi with a bag of chips to purchase

his gym equipment: wheels, extenders, cut-off gloves, works out
until, like the Dying Gaul, his biceps evened out, his stomach, that last

sigh... strained to death, resigned to his gladiatorial demise.
Nor did I ever know, such a shaven-headed convict brute,

a combatant against himself, who swaggers now for walking,
bounces burglars, devours all military invaders to his kingdom,

rents karate movies... sleeps up in the Berg, his horse
tethered to his hand... could ever be so unbearably gentle with me.

He gentles me with his pleasure. Has only one rule: reciprocate. Pleasure
runs best both ways. I say to him, shouldn't you really save this all for

some girlfriend? Has not decided yet. The old excuse: they need money first,
muscles are for men... I'd clean forgot he was staying over once,

occupied all winter about the house in my duties, deadlines, the phone,
stumbled to *my* bed, and there *he* was... for the only bodily

function he can't serve himself. All right then, but turn over.
My knees like muffs about his head. Then again he throttles me to sleep.

Paulus his Brother

But you should see Paulus, his twin. Pick up the phone and
he's on the taxi from Maseru with a packet of crisps.

One must have what the other has, it's only democratic after all,
in our earthly heaven – Sandton City, that shopping mall in the sky!

Drawn to the glittering windows of splendour no one without euros,
dollars can afford. He comes from the poorest land of all,

our neighbouring rough kingdom… steak-eaters without bootstraps, bread,
where everyone's dying even faster. So we have Stephen Gray's

Guide to Safer Sex: lending a hand, find the human being
beneath the machine, no part flaccid or flapping shall obtrude,

roll on this. With Paulus we do an hour's just kissing
to prepare… Whatever his brother does, he does longer,

and vice versa, though they're not identical. Planned
to disarm the body, charm and milk the donor all right.

And when Paulus heaves back into his taxi, with many parcels,
he'll send his next born brother soon, for a bout of Big City spoils.

What else do they have but their superb selves? Wrap up now,
don't show your wallet, go well. A big hug for Marcus, too.

Bernhard the Peace-Monitor

Born after one genocide (Austrian), missing in another (Burundi),
yet so non-aggressive, so tranquil, he didn't even have sex...

thanks to graduate unemployment in Vienna, rather than sing to
his father's cows, with bells round their necks, on snowy old slopes,

came young creamy, blue-eyed Bernhard, six foot six and weighing nix,
to monitor the world's next election scheduled by the U. N.,

in blue uniform, in remotest KZN (the one that saved us).
Completed his doctorate (in English) in my house. From the day gentle

Bernhard arrived my household cat had found her man: covering
long Bernhard's lap on the couch, his feet twitching to the beat

on his private headphones, her tail to the rhythm of his heart.
Their happy idyll. Mine to supply footnotes, forcefeed them both...

Back to that workless waltz in an Alpine boredom... But by 1996
    his address is:
Missions des Nations Unies pour l'Observation des Droits de l'Homme,

B. P. 1490, Bujumbura. With that action station the postal service
is soon suspended. Via New York I hear:
    Every day we get information on more than one

killing. Hardly can follow in filing it down. We are three workers
tracing three million... Mass graves, landmines, local officials

assassinated. There are living dead around, no generator...
    300 returnees
from Zaire killed in a church in Murambi today. We go investigate...

Still I receive your jolly Auslandsösterreicher magazine
with nowhere to forward... Christmas and chocolate rabbits.

I am 30 years now, slowly getting grown up. Unknown
is what caused Bernhard to disappear off this bad earth:

but I know how, limp and long, he'll be laid out to rest.
Close his clear eyes that have seen too much. Check toes for wiggling.

José the Counter-Tenor

From Lisbon, but could have been from any place where opera-singers
practise their deceptive solo-lines in music studios. We were in Tel Aviv

but could have been in any major city where Monteverdi is revived.
By no means castrato these days, but that cultivated high
    girlish vocal range...

Half an hour of scales, he's sweating... All I have to do on the piano is
give him his note... Then I think it's Apollo comforting Orfeo,

after he's turned and lost her to hell. Like bubbles
    atop the fountain-blast,
a line so delicate, for the first time in my life – at such intensity –

I faint... Must have been too many nights ridden out
until the rosy-fingered dawn, etc., on that hairy donkey-dick of his,

that from such a pilltaking, spoilt, pretentious slouch, mildly
crooked, burning the darkness on booze, putting the promise back
    in promiscuity

(I'd been his only ever *three*-night stand), such a hellish debauchee,
could come a song so completely: pure. For applause, I'd slid off
    the stool, out.

Came round, not wanting to make a big scene, carried by students
in the audience to the washroom, damp towels. And later he said,
    from the stench

of his foul, vain lips, "So you like-a my arioso, he loses her, so sad... "
and I could only hold his blue chin and kiss him silent,
    while he thrust at me his artificial song.

Stanley Kiss-and-Tell

From Kimberley arrives Stan the Man, computer-wise
with Standard Eight; otherwise illiterate. Can add:

rands for roses for his sister, cents for chewing-gum –
fortune-seeking, and finds keyboard jobs too, sending surplus home.

Wants my spare room. Will help with the garden, give wobbly
kisses that stick like abalone... He used to chat up a black man

thus, Ou Korrie, would give him a great smacker while he satisfied
himself. No further. In return a jeans suit, two-tone shoes,

once he'd escaped his solemn grandparents down in Griquatown,
what were they, Korannas? Dutch Reformed? On pension? – strict –

bash him with the Bible he can't read. Lying on top, these glossy lads,
feels feminine and good. For an extra grope he nicks a package
    from the fridge.

Why not bring the fiancée up here, sweet Stanza? "Coloured girls
is only pregnant, wanting money", "But Stan, I thought... "

"Only for appearance, kissing don't count. Old Korrie – he's dead now –
gave me leather shirts, tight trousers – who else to provide,
    that was love?"

"Without love it's blackmail." For a job down the railways
    and another smart girl,
he followed his career, taking off that killer smile: firm,

succulent, neat teeth, firm tongue, seductive as a couplet
running on, pay or I'll tell. Hips no touch. Gimme. End-stopped.

Hansie the TV

"Are you looking for someone to talk to… " he whispered, "feeling alone?"
Posed against the bin on the main road, Keep Naboomspruit Clean.

"I'm Hansie and I drink Hansa. Let's go… " What do you want to do?
"Be just a primary teacher in a veld-school now." We stop for his six-pack;

where can we go? You know here, I'm just passing through.
Up in the mountains Rondalia has private rondavels for rent…

Close up his soft brown eye has a smear of liner not creamed away,
chips of pink in the grooves of his thumb. "Took it off for my Ma,

she doesn't like the competition." He is not your average
    Hillbrow hustler,
Skyline transvestite from the deadly old homeland, my dear,

but a major drag artiste. There's no one knows that language out here.
"You should see my ac': I'm jus' alias Diana, after you know who… "

Ross, of course. What happened? I planned we'd be in the bed by then,
but on the floor we fixed the fridge. "Boyfriend worked for BA, threw

me out. Or at least I threw myself out, after eleven whole years,
when I came home and found him, *the bastard*, screwing my girlfriend,

instead of me!" Um, girlfriend? "Yes, just for bringing home,
    it's traditional with blacks."
He honestly had never ever known… Retired from the dirty big city…

The sweet beers were chilled out, the birds bubbling in the thorns,
and dear broken Hansie in my arms kept on pouring out his deep despair

in Naboomspruit where he plays straight and strong. Whimpering now;
with one hand he crushes the can, the other's little finger
    catches a tear.

Prince the Flower-Seller

Whistles while he works, hawking cars at the traffic light
dewy red rosebuds in cellophane, fife ran' a bunch – his only English;

when he needs to top up his bucket of ice with a hose,
mine he borrows, saluting me in my sun-hat damping drought.

On Valentine's Day his grin goes far, flagging down quick-deal lovers
with somewhere to go: fife ran' times fife times…

But with nightfall my doorbell goes: this is him, wants to keep cool
that fourth bucket of tight blooms, before they open up and blow.

Prince he is, has family far outside Ladysmith, only a bed in Soweto:
the Indian has not fetched him, no trains at this streetlamp hour.

Me he offers one last bloom on a long stem, hand nervously shaking, yes,
like a lover on a first date, my Romeo. Hoping to stay over.

My Zulu Prince has a cowskin amulet about his arm, a belt
of blue beads for protection about his waist, around his ankle woven hair;

with these on he sleeps, so that he's never naked, juju to keep him whole:
in bed he will do everything traditional men do, wrestling their prey
    into submission –

bruises, battered flesh, even the purple love bites on my jugular;
this is indeed how he has been taught to satisfy none but himself.

Another time we try some foreplay, isn't that what the roses signify?
Loosening underwear, not ripping them off, custom condoms unrolled,

and my Prince now learns to kiss… stop grunting, more make like a gasp,
more lie back and be ravished than staying hard through a rape.

Once when at last, as he comes across my sweating chest,
    his heave just breaks down
into huge tears, all the lovelessness, homesickness, his manliness
    defeated, pouring out;

and to me at last he is glued past any help, collapsed and viscid
    as a babe.
Our breakthrough in love has been reached. When he goes, he paddles my hand.

Millennium Burn-Artist

"To souls whom love hath robed around with fire"
    – Michelangelo Buonarroti to Tommaso de Cavalieri

At last he'll be honest with me, no lie: I was burning second-degree
during a prison riot… What he omits is who ignited it: himself,

as a means of escape. I say I'm not into human torch, please don't keep
coming inside my life for shelter; take this magic jar, lubricate yourself.

But still there are rough patches he cannot rub (his back), or see
(the charred red behind his ear)… the caress and lick of flame
    and its sore aftermath.

Must be honest, you're the first person I get to love; well, what he
    doesn't explain is why
when my friends come and knock, he's gone by the back door…
    street-prowling again,

setting the pitiless night on fire. Please do not come back,
    don't rely on me,
it's all a con: busking for dinner, snitching the waiter's tip.
    Petty crook.

So fire's your weapon… from a cinder, the long passionate crawl of flame,
first roofs, then floors and dungeons: a rare case of pyromania.

The one the new South Africa never programmed for – no father,
delinquent childhood, mentally disturbed, irredeemable and the last white man:
    all tinder.

Stay away, I'm not into Sunday barbecues of my kind, fellow citizens,
stab him and the fat spurts. With his cigarette, singeing his wrist-hair.

Lock him up and he'll unlock the elements: safekeep earth,
    store water and air,
but he'll hold the fire again, a brazier to warm himself by,
    a lousy circus stunt.

See, I exhale hot apocalypse, lighting the fuse… see the special effect,
how I glow alight, how I spark, how I draw even you with my fiery kiss…

May he heal now, shiny with Baby Oil… regress, be reborn…
Backrubbed and shagged out. Please stop that Judgement Day.
    His blush of being burnt.

Henno the Diver

This is the hard one now: handyman Henno who stoked up, lifted off, dived
to his oblivion, from a building-site, head first, flailing...

his wife had quit him for the local cop, who left on stone
in chalk the outline of his impact, removed his poor corpse.

Twenty-six, with a five-year-old daughter and, as it happens, his only son
on the way, safely adopted by the SAP. Disabled by mourning,

his drunken brother enacted for me the rush: mouth calling, legs kicking,
this jobless suicide, also cheated in love. Over the top, my Henno.

For me he was routine household verbs: mowing, fixing, guarding, turning,
cooking over, washing up, bedding down, *ek sorg vir jou*, must phone.

Here in my home nothing worked without Henno: picking, bottling the plums
and peaches in syrup, our poor man's Christmas bounty: old Boer habits.

He had honeyblond unruly hair, the bluest eyes, tanned without freckles,
a perfect top dental plate (could afford no fillings, had them out);

featherweight league, fractured septum, soon spat blood, sinus,
weather-beaten in summer, pleasing to the eye of softer older women
    and those dubious uncles

of suburbia who invited him in – Klipdrift and Coke, Luckies, boom,
pummelling in the dark, all varieties of bodily chore. Liked being watched.

This he became proficient at: serving the more his wondrous, curving, whip-
lash rangy flesh, while the rest of his world went out of control.
    Just love

kept him alight amid what darkness (12 million unemployed to death,
15 million hapless searching for fathers to chastise them with the staff).

Before he'd filled the bath with blood, the blue vein in his wrist
    cut with broken glass;
he took poison and pills; sewn up and pumped out in emergency;
    the usual cries for help.

Always he walked back to me; grew dim; KOed; there was no further
    motivating him;
finally punished himself (and all those he left behind).
    Last fall into the grave.

I. and J. Leave for the Big Apple

Rarely in our love-world will it rain; living in the dry land
where rape and drying out, abuse and salt go hand in hand:

but here encoded come these other two scions of different houses,
whom I recollect once fog becomes drizzle becomes soaking:

for they are the Jew clasps Gentile, that holy book of prohibitions,
     the Torah,
meets its match – the Koran. All ways so Levitically verboten.

And neither knew just what to do with their other, met at the MBAs
     after class…
drove up Kloof Nek, confessed over that now world famous gay friendly

southern spread where even the oceans meet: "I think something terrible
has happened, I cannot help it, I've taken advice: I've fallen in love –
     with another man."

"And so have I." But the years of shame and counselling did pass,
while avoiding themselves, each other, they could never confess:
     they were the one.

By which time I. was a Woolworths manager, and J. consulted,
out at Old Mutual, on website glitches. At last asweat,
     over coffee, stuttering:

compatible. Misty-eyed. Their first expression together
     that could be called sexual,
behind the lighthouse near the all-night drive-in, catching up.
     And double milkshakes.

Now outside their family circles we know them as inseparable
as I. & J. (the fish-firm), the mix-and-match buddies, that pair

who mope even if they're in different rooms, they've grown like each other's
underwear: intimate as organ-donors, like the Bible says: same clay,

same breath. On Holy Days their separate dynasties *still* parade before them
hopeful brides to convert them back to breed. But they're fast now as H_2O...

Rain into air. Salt into sea. Lava into rock. They interpenetrate,
are chemically combined, etc. Hating our old violence,
    they decide to emigrate.

MY NAME IS JAMIE

MY NAME IS JAMIE. IN SOUTH HILLS IS NO WORK.
CAN I CUT YOUR GRAS AND GARDEN, TIDY NICE? –

I HAVE NO JOB, BUT TAKE A COFFEE SO LONG? – (NODS) –
WITH SUGAR? – (TWO FINGERS) – MILK? – A SPLASH.

(PATS HIS CHEST, MEANS GRATITUDE) – NOW TELL ME,
JAMIE, WHO ARE YOU? WHY SELECT ME? WHY NOW?

I AM JAMIE O'BRIEN, MY GRANDFATHER IRISH, NOT
CATHOLIC!! – THEN WHAT? – APOSTOLIC SORRY, NEED BREAD.

I CHOOSE YOU BECAUSE SOUTH HILLS IS NOT ANY WORK FOR HANDYMAN,
SEE THROUGH YOUR GRILLE HYDRANGEAS MUST CUT BACK AND MULCH.

I'M NOT AN EMPLOYER, HAVE MY WORK TO DO AND MOW
MY OWN LAWN, YOU SEE. – (STARES BLUE-EYED, DISAPPOINTED,

SMACKS HIS RIBS) BUT I CAN DO BETTER (PASSES
THE PAD... SECOND THOUGHT) SOM MONEY FOR CHRISTMAS...

(BITES THE PEN, LOOKS GUILELESS) PRESENTS FOR MY TWO
BOYS, WIFE NO WORK, MUST EARN (ADDS), SIR.

I ALMOST ASK, DO THEY FLAIL AS WELL, TIE A KNOT
IN THE AIR AND PUNCH IT AWAY? THEIR PRIVATE MIME?

JAMIE, WHERE DID YOU LEARN? – SPECIAL SCHOOL FOR DEAF
AND DUMB, RUSTENBURG WHEST. (ZIP ZIP THE SIGNALS.)

HE PUTS BETWEEN HIS TEETH A BISCUIT, HEARS NO CRACK
AND CRUNCH AND SWALLOW DOWN. DOES NOT KNOW SOUND.

SO HEARS BY TOUCH. I TOUCH HIS NOSE, CHEEKS, CHAPPED UNDERLIP. –
YOU'RE VERY SUNBURNT. IN SUMMER WHEN BEGGING WEAR A HAT. –

WE'RE BEYOND NOTES. HE MOUES AS I SMOOTH SUNBLOCK,
PURSES FOR GREASE, HOLDS HIMSELF STIFF, TRUSTING ME:

THERE NOW, PROTECTED… THE CLEAREST WAY TO SAY IT
IS TO HUG. WE HUG. INTO HIS WORN FIST I PUSH HIS TIP.

BUT THIS IS NOT FAREWELL. TO THE SINK HE TAKES HIS MUG,
AS IF HE BELONGS HERE. TURNS REGRETFULLY. ANOTHER EMBRACE.

HE PICKS UP HIS CARDBOARD NOTICE, UNDERLINES:
MY NAME IS JAMIE O'BRIEN FROM SOUTH HILLS, NO WORK,

GRANDFATHER IRISH, TWO GROWING BOYS TO SUPPORT:
LOOKS UP, CURLY-HAIRED, STROKES HEART. *THANK YOU*

FOR ALL ASSISTANCE. GOD BLESS YOU AND HAVE A NICE DAY.
GO WELL TOO (I WRITE), AND EVERYTHING GREAT FOR YOU. LAST HUG.

Nuru the Peddler's Christmas

Raffish and spindleshanked, splay-footed, young Nuru
from Somalia, whose warlords still fight across his turf;

takes refuge from a far country; these, Ibn Battutah
on his travels called the best barterers for Allah.

His forehead's high, white teeth apart for sieving mangos
or whistling up the camel-train, darkest, far-glinting eyes

scan savannah. On our Main Reef Road makes salaam;
for whom most unimaginable First World luxuries are by law haraam.

At the traffic light's red with bandoliers of headsets,
Gluestix, baseball caps and balls and phoney Rolexes:

an African totem flailing into all grin, accepts coin
through the rolled-down, tinted window, genuflects, counts:

and it's green again. As yet he is without our sophisticated tongue,
talks of *money-banki, ricey, banana, tree-mun extenshun*.

With no other papers, like 20 000 here he has refugee status.
Taught to higgle and chaffer, truckling, he knows each price.

Now he's rising in the streets, young Nuru visits me
for English lessons, like a connoisseur downs just one beer.

For his limpid mother in a creased photo back home he sends
his savings, still a good son, unentitled to respect and adult sex.

On Sunday afternoons he polishes his mountain bike,
checks his store of hardwon goods, polishes Nikes,

is ready for snooker. The gangly arm, the lethal eye, line up.
When he spills his dreams, its more mangos, rice, at last his own wife…

Outside the crowded parlour our great police at Christmas
snatch him, dropping a can into the bin: public nuisance,

although he's never drunk. Lock him up for our Feast of the Nativity.
After haggling, for the usual bribe they release him.

Filthy, beaten up, on the pane he taps at 5.00 a. m. the 26th,
says it's nothing at all, crawls into bed, quivers, quivers.

* * *

Alternative Route

So this is what I wish for:
a turn-off from the N1, a route without number,
cambered well with only mild corrugations
setting up a rhythm, never monotonous.
My Firestones bite, mountains ahead –
far ranks of rolling blue, impenetrable –
with baggy ostriches in dusty disarray
claiming back the desert for their flock,
with warning signs: sheep, kudu jumping –
no other vehicles… that iron sunflower,
the windmill churning up the planet's rust
and few plants. Only a thorn-tree, with yellow
bobbles in the sun's slaty brown, brown.
With cattlegrids beside concertina gates,
and telephone poles for kestrels to build
their fine lookouts: for this is vermin country,
to be patrolled, with hefty, swaying dust-devils.
And names like Blaauwkrantz, Syferfontein,
and a watercourse called Gamka, that once a century
floods everywhere – so that my last trace
is a smooth)(aftertow! across the vlei
of these scrubby mirrored flats, that closes
behind me as I am gone…
And by nightfall I must be bursting uphill
towards the flagrantly coloured sky.

Singing Dunes

During the Christmas road-kill, the declining matric results,
    Witsand endures past all our millennia,
The record rape statistics of girlfriends, grans, daughters,
    Violence on mothers and their burst children,
Pipe-bombs under pizza-eaters and mounting billions of fraud,
    Witsand endures, these handfuls of sand…
Windborn, deposited, saved on the great savannah, compounding,
    A secret dune floating on its own reservoir,
While the closed-theatre, stolen-car, poison-watered days
    Pass through your palms like broken glass
And the dumps of dirt on bankrupt streetcorners accumulate
    Where fiery trees once grew, rinsing air:
At Witsand time itself is pure, no classical hit-parade at Witsand,
    Even iron is leeched with moisture, bright skies,
While this radio for the ill-informed, ever wondered who to turn
    To for investment advice, poisoned apples to bite –
At Witsand hear the layers shift, the whisper of the very stones…
    Every microlith chipped, each shard a fingerpad
And the desert grind into granules through that final hour-glass
    Scratching at your earlobe. Better luck
Next time, grit is all you ever were, ground to dust… so take care,
    While Witsand endures singing of transformation and of waste.

Hoopoe

With your pharaoh's crest, fine feathers
spattered in fertile mud, decurved beak;
favoured among Chosen People, I hear,
to carry messages of state from Africa
to King Solomon from Sheba your queen.
Never mind his wisdom, her spices and gold,
as the Bible states in I Kings.
We're talking secrets of big dealers
and how you pried in to read her last P. S.
Something you know, as you probe my lawn,
go "Hoop oop, shekel! Hoop oop, shekel!"

The Black Eagles of Roodekrans
(for Gordon Dickerson)

"Nowhere in the world would such wild things,"
you said over the Sunday buffet, "nest like that
in an urban area." "They were here first,"
I replied, scanning from the lawn to the waterfall,
enclosed in their rust-red strata, where their
thrown-together habitat is on closed-circuit TV:
for raptor-watchers, that is picnickers at peace
in the Botanical Gardens, unclenched and sunbathing.
Lucky to catch the upright black mother preen on a tree,
while her smaller mate surveys for tomorrow's prey.
December is chick time: two hatched apart
into their first contest, a white muddle
of quill and beak needing to kill, one the other,
the victor spattered into yolk and a brother's blood:
hail Cain! Cain clean up the vermin! flex your wings!
destined to a great campaign and hell on dassies. "What's a dassie?"
"Like rock-rabbits, basking in the kloofs, but these days
our birds-of-prey have to cruise a few countries off
for a clean swoop." Peripherally we think we see
a thick, angular shadow, push our plates aside,
drain beer. Up the crest just jumbled twigs,
the tiny plunge that feeds the mighty Limpopo, barbed
wire to keep us off. "There's a Verreaux's Eagle
Fan Club," I say, "feeds them hares from the abattoir.
Too much gate-money would be lost if they pushed off."
We pant, wipe sweat, digest a bit, share sweets.
Then you made first sighting, while I fumbled with binoculars:
that black immense wingspan, the white V displayed like a hinge
holding the shoulders, the hooked snout, yellow marble eye,
gliding… and there now, the two-is-a-pair, testing for take-off…
"Well spotted, Gordon." Must be your British instincts
for bombing raids and Spitfires, keeping a weather eye out,

cringing under sky. Our hazards here in Africa we keep
more underfoot: snakes that must be rooted out, crocodiles,
feral dogs to pounce on, rats that pour with refugees.
"You said golden plumage, more tawny… " So, bracketed
between them, there comes the fledgling immature, out
on its first aerial manoeuvre: gawky, can't take
the curves with that always graceful calculation yet,
but aloft now, determined to stay up. We run along the path
through sugarbushes, as if we thundering mortals
could ever come close… and then we stand transfixed.
Now the temperature, the time is right, for that updraft
to lift them higher – 5 kilos she soars with her 2 metre
wingspan, and her partner curving in the slipstream. Between them
their shrieking, giddy, baffled birdbrain. Has to learn.
Paragliding, or rather a spiral in a flight-path
destined to infinity, towards that vast cumulus on high…
three specks, like an ellipsis, in the lens.
Then even around once more, specks in endless pure blue,
becoming too minute for human vision as they persist in
their immaculate ascent.

Lake Asal

This is the land where fingerlings in a boiling
cauldron do not cook, their camels cross
fields of salt, bearing bags of salt grains,
driven by these nomads, out of the rift to the
civilised uplands for barter, where gypsum
and halite are all there is to open-mine
from the raging volcanic circle, and we step
into immensity like Arthur Rimbaud, yes,
below sea-level... in procession away from
every thing green, plush, plentiful into infinite
haze... cuts do not heal at Lake Asal:
salt opens the wound, your body bleeds, you blanch,
you cover in crystal, like this sheep-skull
encrusted the lad is winking his
Swatch at me for, to trade as a memento
of this valley of chloride, of steam, of mirage:
his hair is salt spikes, flesh sprinkled, his
teeth when he grins are shocking: filed to points
like a shark's, guarded by goat-smell, eyes red from glare;
he has come to regard us, as we tourists do to view him:
but this is his world, unimaginable to my kind
as, to him, is a shore, a ship, a banquet-hall,
where his mutton would serve and salt be kept in cruets
for seasoning the done flesh that we rush back to devour.

* * *

Room Service

He must when he catwalks the quay
sway his skirted hips and all,
have a chain about his glossy neck
tied with a paperclip, be that tall;

and if at the tiller his dhowish craft
bucks currents, his hand be firm and fair;
when diving, his full lips about the snorkel,
emit from his wide nostrils slow air;

and chop the pearl-caskets free,
with a ring of salt his anklet catching;
none other should he be, who knocks
for me some nights. Come in, Ibrahim.

Or if it's now his brother, black moustached,
who calls so late and whispers Mohamed,
that's expected in these immoral bays;
shy and shaken, he'll also fall into bed.

Yet with Ibrahim – his sloping chest, his scars,
his briny glasses and broken vest –
our fondness grows, a drop into a Red Sea,
a kind of edgy, secure affection, unprofessed.

Engulfed, I seize his heavy breath,
the probing knuckles never meant to
crack me like an oyster – ah my fine one –
and slurp me up. Please enter.

Whoever raps had better be that dextrous,
must run his curls across my chin,
have at least that swaying walk,
waist, chain-link, or I'll never let him in.

Body Language

Once you're asleep your body
talks for you, my arm round your navel
and up it rises, on the bone
of my wrist smallest kisses.

Or else it's you enfolding me
snug as teaspoons, they once said,
and then you're my Fidelity Guard
baton in the small of my back.

Like a scout always prepared
with this metronome of your heart
ticking away your dirty dreams,
"This is a stick-up, boy."

One night I'll keep watch,
count the times you climb up
out of that soggy, melting warmth
that grows between us both –

or while you're off wet-dreaming
elsewhere, it's all the same:
but this is the hand that holds your heat,
milks the stream of your desire.

I'll sneak the headphones on
to hear your secret bodypart,
restless the night long like
an old lady making her camomile,

"You should have seen that bird-
fancy boy stroke his plum-head,
and I said I've a cockatoo on show,
we should get together."

And after that flying combat
over you turn and snore again,
my middle finger down your thigh,
"Oh sorry" you murmur and swallow…

but then you're back for more,
nose in my ear, lips wet,
knotted up in the placket
your cock through your boxers

and behold you need your nurse,
your nanny crawling out
from the unbelievable bulk,
the load of all of you.

Such friction between us
generates sharp static,
that's when I know you love me
or anyone else who'll comfort you so.

Erections like that are infectious,
you start one and I catch it, and
next thing every single male in town
is off and out, looking for a place to go…

On waking you groan to lose
that fleshy bond for two,
get your crotch back down
and in and under your own control.

"Morning, stranger," I greet,
"I thought I knew you well,
But human speech is really a screen
behind which you never can tell."

He is a man of no words,
snaps his toothbrush, spits,
taking his coffee the hair on his knuckle
rises to touch the hair on mine.

And through the day there's a part
of me stiffens of its own accord,
reaching for you in our other world
too dark ever for us to express.

Proposal

I am not, repeat not, one who falls in love
that often, in fact it's a long while since I have;

the frequency's arranged in heaven, while propinquity
on earth encourages the chance to see, grab, hold, agree;

this practice needs no theory, in case of action we rehearse;
the knuckle opportunity keeps tapping; I'm tapping back – yes, *repeat* yes;

that was the affirmative, your battery must be running flat;
well, read my posture then, the last chance is where we're at;

oh you thought I meant roses; um, they are very fine;
roses rise to the occasion every time; no, *rise, shine*… ah never mind.

Knock, knock. "Who's there?" Jane. "Which Jane?" Ag, skip it;
in your bathrobe at this restless hour – it'll only take a minute.

Digest, divest, itsy-bitsy at the flowing palace-pool;
women wrap, they say, ooze silently; only man's the bidden bulging fool.

* * *

Mad Poet in His Tower
(Friedrich Hölderlin *loq.***)**

Poor lost Hölderlin, in me the natural elements are now changed forever,
where old logic and God flowed, that river water cooled, I am skated upon.

Das Feld ist kahl... the only phrase above my jingling metal bed
on which I am tied down, X-shaped, gagged for my loss of faith,
     sorely scarred –

but saved from what I have to suffer, your kitsch daffodils and willows,
     your terrible church-bells...
children punting, my manuscripts their paper-boats, these striped pyjamas...

confined in this their tower, my brilliant demons tranquillised, dissolved –
     then I may stomp
down the straight corridor and up the winding stair, I am grain ground
     to bran to bread.

Yes I too believed in that revolution when even all our loathsome Fritzes
and Wilhelms were welcome back to the human race, preferably headless –

when women would rule without restraint: she rides me, bites my
     needle-pointed bleeding tits,
shoves her rigid sceptre up my arse – just like any man, you see –

when the lion lay with yet another lamb – and joined those yellow teeth
about the throat, and throttled it, to lick up again its jewelled crown.

Beware of peasants gorging sausages, made of dripping cows' vaginas,
and drinking beer which is bull's piss, they fertilise together
     and become cloven-hoofed –

to an ox I am reduced, so that you feed me, groom me, toil alongside
as I plough your muddy grave; between my crossed eyes hammer a nail.

You walk me across another battlefield, pick off the ripe soldiers
		their paired testes
like cherries, spit the stones: in us their genes must live on – communion –

and now I can stride, outpace you, look: Tübingen… Toledo… Timbuktu…
all Africa, have I not written that: Love brought forth new millenniums? –

there they are all ignorant masses, but I see so beautiful: only they
		with new laws will survive
to that Second Age. I have given up hope for my tuba-playing people
		these forty years

confined in my tower, where postcolonial punks spray hateful slogans
and tourists stupidly pay to touch-my-mad-elbow. And voilà, I am
		no longer here,

I am gas, I am in the air you breathe: on your nosehairs I pollute
		and coalesce
like grime, become your catarrh and as you swallow hard – feel, I freeze.

On a Lock of Pushkin's Hair

Chestnut glinting, curly not crissy, romantically
Circled in a bow… traces of arsenic to cure syphilis,
Evidence of the octoroon negro-look, but only fractionally,
More a hank round the little finger, a riming kiss.

Stroked on pillows, by the conquests of Don Juan bit at,
Upright at old ghosts… under sheepskin over versts, a serf shaved
In exile, tugged at for African roots… in summer the straw-hat…
Petted and cut by a tsar, shorn by admirers at the grave.

Spirit of a new land, sprouting irrepressible, unruly,
Lived losing, made neat poetry, gestural of pains,
Combed out from chaotic, rolling fun this one truly
Sparse lock of lines, this hitch of hair, his scalped remains.

On the Body of Ché Guevara

Message to the Bolivian miners:
"Patiently we prepare
for the deep-going revolution
that will transform the system
from top to bottom" –
that without goodwill, without supplies,
will never happen.
On 9 October 67,
his body like a false Jesus
on a stretcher is displayed.
His diary of the guerilla campaign
is published as propaganda.
But he could not keep his compadres
together. A doctor unable
to fix even his own asthma.
Remember the birthdays of his
own children not yet stroked.
Notes how he has failed.
His last choice: the martyr's way.
Prays for the right assassin.
Bites the bullet.

On Hannibal, General
(after Juvenal, Satire X)

Consider glorious Hannibal: how more in the end did he weigh
than his raging body? The man whom all his continent
could not contain, from the Moorish sea to the hot Nile,
all Ethiopia and its elephants, he of the scorpion-strike.
Adds to his kingdom Spain, overleaps the Pyrenees,
sleeps in his cloak among his troops, leaves all battles last.
Then in his howdah, lion-shielded, scars to the fore,
leads his hundred thousand over the Alps of snow,
cleaving the very rock; to possess all Italy he swarms down.
"Nothing," he vows, "is done until my Carthage
bursts their gate to plant our standard there."
What a rich spectacle, that one-eyed stoic general,
his kinky, flaming hair – the African who conquered Rome!
Behind his back the base he as a boy, keen for carnage,
had meant to save, sixteen years before, is taken.
To shelter he flees in another's shade, a fretting exile –
the liberator of an empire, fallen into wounded age.
Once the world was stirred never to be the same again,
by Hannibal Barca, whom no sword but his own might pierce.
How vain are human wishes! He is mere flesh for a ransom!
Just so that we may declaim all his lost deeds,
sing his praise-song for ever, with no mention of his defeat.

An African Elegy
i. m. Léopold Sédar Senghor (1906–2001)

The French West African poet, whose long sad lines
    unpunctuated pattered rhythmically on and on,
imprisoned by Saxons in stalags, fighting for those Celts,
    their representative black citizen,
praised the unknown tirailleur of Senegal dying for his freedom in Wolof,
    buried silent, man among men,
who glossed us non-speakers his terms:
    Mogador, harmattan, saudades, medina, balafong.

Beside the malice of burn, baby, burn,
    he clutched his missal of dark nocturnes,
longed for a prodigal return to that Garden of Tribal Childhood,
    wrote for the academy the classical ode, the sprung and
    heartfelt elegy
on Kaya-Magan to King Shaka, Alexandria to the Cape,
    the Seine flooding right down to the great Zambezi:
poet of vain longing, for dialogue his surreal catalogue,
    for his lost continent of silt forever he yearns.

As president did one wholly trust those steel-rimmed specs,
    the half-smile always looking askance,
dropped his totems for totalitarian means, made Marxism over
    to the market, banned his opposition,
proclaimed his duty was exactly to measure that field, share the harvest
    out, forgetting neither workers nor orphans.
From the 81 conference we telegrammed a salute, for setting the example,
    to resign at the end of his term.

In retirement he meant to synthesise antithesis, remarked we are all
    of us *métis* now, must shake hands, interdepend.
Pacified himself, translating the conservatives, Yeats and Eliot and Hopkins
    and even old spent Dylan Thomas, to the end.

On the Grave of Sarah Baartman

So this is where she was born, though we cannot be sure:
     "Master gaan so en so, dan oppie koppie and up,
meneer"… where the toposcope radiates our joint history
     in mixed syllables: Tsitsikamma, Milton, Cambria,
Rooivlakte there, and this named after a Scottish banker Hankey…
     where the world's biggest dial points aloft
to the mighty sun climbing to its precise perihelion.
     This closed Gamtoos Valley with orange orchards, neat
as corduroy, the stubby tobacco sliced into pipes and lit…
     What would she recognise, before the Mfengus
and the LMS? A stalking rainbird summoning this peaceful motrain,
     the zik-zik-zik of a ruby-red bishop
on reeds feathering, those scarlet paths winding off and away
     into fynbos, with proteas, with noisy hadedahs,
mimosa bobbles… Now among agaves, silver roofs reflect
     the clouds, through a patch of potatoes runs
the rackety railway… no tree she's ever swung from,
     just bougainvillaea and jacaranda
and spreading gums that infest and suck up the brak and burn off:
     perhaps a sour euphorbia patch, there by
Ruiters Funeral Parlour, beyond the low commercial hotel.
     Under lights that signal anti-crime
the township huts with square eyes and a vertical mouth
     for a door, the pensioner seated and throwing a scrap
to a beaten African dog, the one which never barked
     at her: his ou Saartjie, returned at last.
And with such official pomp! The whole new risen state!
     Come to her funeral, the sportsfield crammed:
an icon they address her as, over which we have to reconcile!
     This showbiz girl, this famous human specimen!
Surveying all, her grave is above her abused geography,
     the urgent agribusiness, the rich and heavy-drinking poor,

behind security bars, in case her body's stolen yet again,
    her casket's weighed with offerings: "Thank you,
Mrs Baartman, that we love one another." A vetplant
    in Christmas wrapping. An engraved stone. A medal.
The vygies and the prickly pears with septic fingers,
    the aloes wearing plastic bags, all point,
above energy drinks and condom wrappers, to this humble wayside
    cairn, where she lies, safely after centuries, at rest.
Above her a million butterflies detach, launch off and
    go migrate, as she did, tender and pretty and all
too soon broken, past the mast and scanner of our Skywave
    Galaxy, listening in these days for news of an astronaut.
Salute her, where you stand in dignity – our little sister –
    for she is home once more, the ceremony complete.

Chain Letter

When you receive this poem kiss someone you love
And make sure they kiss those first-class they love too.
Beloveds are eligible, but also elderly and children,
Even those many, many people who cannot read this in English.
Copies of this poem have been round the planet
Ninety times – so, a great chain of human kisses.
Also try to kiss those you don't love so much:
Otherwise no luck, chain is for ever broke.
Within four days of kissing your awful next-door neighbour
You will receive good luck right down the street…
The chain starts with Saint Anthony de Group,
A missionary in Venezuela who was granted full remission.
Let your secretary send twenty copies out
And you get a new VW Citi Golf 1-point 6 Sports.
Miss Ama Prescott of Mmabatho got running-water,
Robot-maid, free cruise and many kisses for the first time.
The poem says dry-lip kiss only, not lick suck
Swallow something not your own, so keep population down.
Mail all copies of this poem out now to friends and associates,
Increase the chance Lady Luck comes in your post.
Copy faithfully by Rank or Nashua – typing mistakes
Like *hit* your neighbour cause World War again
Without jackpot bonanza big cash-cascade
Payout… just no rice, no tea, potatoes, bananas.
The original of this chain-poem is kept in a casket
Sealed up in Nagasaki, 100% nuclear-bomb-proof
For all these decades and E equals my-love squared:
Nowadays the whole universe must kiss and kiss or else…
Send no money. Do not ignore this poem, it works!

Hippo
(after Théophile Gautier)

The hippo with its bulging belly
lives on our stretches of damp savannah,
where echo in caverns, ripe and smelly,
undreamed of sheaves of Africana.

While the python uncoils itself and hisses,
the leopard makes its spotty cry
and the buffalo's tail is up and pisses,
hippo blows bubbles, or grazes tranquilly.

Never he dreads the kris or assegai,
before any scholar he'll hold his ground,
the native's bullets pass him by
for off his leather hide they all rebound.

I am like that hippopotamus,
formed by my private, my own inner drive,
grown armoured, if a bit ridiculous,
unafraid to tread the riverbank and dive.

Learning Italian
(for Itala Vivan)

Midway in my life's journey I have paid up and signed,
study my Lezioni di Grammatica per Principianti.
With "essere – indicativo presente" we commence our lesson.

"Perchè siete in Italia?" – "Io sono in Italia per studiare
la lingua italiana." By Intermedio I manage an essay:
"La Mia Casa": "Al momento abito in una casa

vicino della città di Johannesburg in mio paese,
Sudafrica. Questa bella casa è la mia." Bravo!
On to Conversazione… It's a long haul to Paradise.

On Those Learned Quills

TASSO:
Of valiant Vasco, whose brave mast was raised to the pole,
steered off for the rising sun and returned where it sets,
you pen, O brave Luigi, your Spanish inky jets,
an epic more soaring than a navigator's goal.

CAMOENS:
For Portugal, you mean, I travelled far and sold my soul,
not for your Italian Polo the world forgets,
for Da Gama's fame and fortune I ran up all my debts,
poetry's no just reward, as you must know, on the whole.

DA GAMA:
O Tasso, the route you scribble out was followed by Columbus,
nor any Cyclops did I provoke, but African Adamastor,
lashed by rope and tongue, the brute I made adore,
as for Harpies, all whores, no sonnet but a blunderbuss.

ADAMASTOR:
Hail bombastic poets, hail bragging Vasco in soft doublet,
all you may command are words, words to fill a couplet.

Translating Montale

He inhales. "Not Montale," gruffly, "for a South African
he is too difficult." Exhales… "Even for us professors.

Wish one you want translate? 'I Limoni' – very early Montale…
What class are you? So-called Advanced, after only two years

– Typical Italian exaggeration, to be kind to foreigners –
Montale of the twenties is hell: im-pos-si-bi-le!" Stubs out.

On a terrace before the lake we are above the lemon-trees in question,
along from here that first difficult impossible poem took place.

About their scent in a doorway (I figure), wet footprints on tiles,
two of their fruit nobbled beneath a downy damp towel.

Or on a wooden board, chopped. Sunlit and scratchy.
Slung above those fertilising northern trenches. Who really knows? –

in Europe from doorknobs one conjures a castle, from pediments
forums of columns, whole temples from a sole pagan bone.

So I must retreat to unbroken Africa… plod on more at the Dante
Alighieri Society to Conversazione I, II, III

in what those Fascists called Johannesburgo, where their prisoners
-of-war were poorly skilled, unable to read what they most desired:

their own Montale. But a fellow of mine, Patrick, after years
of study and application, managed just that: to translate Montale,

except for 'I Limoni', surely too obscure to bring off well.
Yet I have brave cribs of it by Brandeis and Kay, more or less

accurate, and on order the definitive facing version by Galassi.
Understanding all the words literally, we know, is only the start:

Listen to me; the laureate poets walk only among those bushes
with seldom used names: box-wood or acanthus. Dante himself, I take it,

and that pompous D'Annunzio, the rare verses of whom
our very patient teacher, dear Grazia, recites to shut us up:

just listen to them, good God, for theirs is how high language
    was invented
to go, approved by many Parliaments and (even if he's not Italian)
    the Pope,

but Montale, Montale, as he says (and this much I do fully
understand, and endorse): went elsewhere. Drifted off the syllabus…

Those lemon-trees, gnarled, spiky, dug in through that long bad time
for rhetoric and human rights, so ordinary they can be overlooked.

But to translate a single Montale, I know, one must translate all
Montale – nothing less will serve, to learn his temper and his turns,

that rhythmic floorplan of grooved stones from which
one should reconstruct (in this case I realise) *his* true world.

"Never fear the exact text," I plead with Grazia, "context is all:
and how can I not make room there for *our* point of view?"

"But that's the problem," she explained, bangle to forehead,
"he's a pure hermetic," she said, without the 'h', "not meant

to be hunderstood heven by Italians… we can do pizza, we can do
Pasolini and Alitalia, prosciutto, Aida, finocchio, Agip,

but Montale, ah no… you make-a a beeg mistake:
Nobel Prize, 1975, everybody knows they gave him the benefit

of the doubt; but otherwise when it's Ferrari and Fiat and fettucine
and Garibaldi and the new Lamborghini, I tell you, Montale's out!"

None the less we attempted just one, simpler, that came out an all-South
African disaster: around a velodrome a charge of... what, buffaloes?

"Ah yes," I snorted: "Futurism! the drop handle-bars
of racing-bikes. And spot the jackals, scorpions, storks

migrating for our pristine Cape, the burnt wadis of Hitler's
vile false spring. How else to write at all under such censorship?"

And Grazia, understandably not wishing to recall her blighted past,
conceded, well, typical Montale it may be, but *minor* Montale.

Came the closing of the school and indeed, yes, I was now due
to win the prize for my year (I was the only one left, to be exact);

there were no other certified translators of verse, and shaking like a leaf –
bay or box or humbly lemon – I unrolled before them,

to pay my tribute, my final version of Eugenio Montale's
'The Lemon-trees' (African style), on the Highveld, in liberated 1998 –

December to be precise, after a rapid thunderstorm
covering the Venetian red corrugated roofs in cocktail ice,

tugged the last of the jacaranda blossoms, causing the mike
to go fuzzy before me: I gave it to them, plain and clear.

He knew the glorious path (he said), but followed another. A poor lad
feeds on muddy eels, only the birds are free: man deeply suffers.

In the market most provisions cost too much, only the lemons
are cheap, but lemons are bitter, sour, their sickly, clinging

scent is cheaper still… And then, lost in the atrocious city of
noise and dirt, I become incoherent, as he did, become

incomprehensible even to myself… but they do grasp each word, because
they are not listening to me at all, they are hearing through me

Montale translated – "greasy perfume on the fingers"… "memory"…
the degraded, the inhuman: "Yellow, now golden" their

shall we say "sunburst"? – sharp as a squirt in the eye.
And I have done it, at last. Silence. Then applause. I accept

my prize: what can it be? – a small jug after all, for fresh
milk from the udder. Bowing and thanking, I run for my car –

when out of that glowing cumulus comes a hoary voice, I swear,
speaking what else but Italian, warning me to beware

of breach of copyright, permission from the estate and (in sum)
    demanding:
was I *authorised*, did I know what Farrar, Straus had had to pay?

To which I replied, "Frankly no, Mr Montale. Who can compute
what the Italian Renaissance, and your Modernism too, is worth

to the entire world? And what the hell *did* that last sentence mean,
    anyway?"
The master grew stern. "Ees jus' to annoy you," he explained

(in English), "because some time the people do not wish to be provoke."
Such a necessary tactic. And I bless old Montale now whenever

I offer do you take it with white, or perhaps just a taste of
lemon, pure as a teardrop? Fragrant. Beyond all rendering.

* * *

Shelley Cinema

I

Shelley's dead; for Mary the weeping –

How did they cut out his heart?

You say an apple you
    offer me,
but this is red and soft
    and fries well,
a tomato; you say an apple
    but this is a peach;
a peach and a tomato are not
    that apple and all it signifies.

(On 11 September 2001 in Rapallo
looking for memorabilia of E. Pound,
I heard the news of the planes bombing
the two World Trade towers
and the Pentagon on the phone from Milan –)

This is the way the old world ends (or some such);
welcome to our new century.

In Shelley Cinema we have –
    live footage of his drowning
of Mary's weeping
of Lord Byron driving
    the knife between his ribs
    to excise his heart (oh yes).

Say Shelley's body is burning
    on the beach in a pyre –
the World Trade towers
    collapse in the heat
    upon him, implode
    about his hearty lungs,
but for the thousands of dead
    his heart is saved.

His anarchist heart
    is dripping in the Americas.
(The chapel bells toll at Bellagio too,
    over the twin lakes,
and rowing together comes
    the wooden barque
from which he fell and drowned!)

On the beach Lord Byron burns
    the twin towers of his limbs,
the pentagon of his skull burns,
    his circuits are fused
and all his intelligence.

In this hazy retreat
    where patrons propose and dispose,
the late news is Shelley the Poet
    is dead from drowning
and New York City smells of mourning.

For Mary the weeping has also only
    just begun, her widowhood,
the charred papers to order
    and edit and assemble for sale,
her only dowry and inheritance.

With our lenses we invade her face,
    the red dust and sticky lashes,
behind Mary the widow's Raybans

  for the twin towers she weeps
and into the merciless, sour sea

that sucked down Shelley for whom breath
  was more than life,
was man's freedom in a new world
  and woman's mourning in the old –
dry of oxygen and waterlogged with salt,

weeping for the twin towers of his manliness,
  the sweet melodious throat
of his metrical breath and the kiss
  of his sweet lips, O
Shelley is dead in the Poets' Bay.

Over a lunch with the capitalist
  working for the World Bank
who likes to control this earth
  which cannot be controlled –
only spoilt, but not possessed –

he said he heard Shelley was dead
  at last, and so that was that –
no more the terror of anarchy
  and the blast in the night:
American Airlines heading for…

He was relieved in his castle,
  grew salad in his moat, allowed there
soccer for the village lads rather than
  acts of exertion with bombs
to hurl us along to paradise!

The bells toll noon over Lerici
  and Mary is off her food,
the scent of her husband's burning
  like a barbecue
means she will never be eating again,

not at the restaurant or at McDonald's
      where mashed cow vulvas are sold
as honest meat, where the clam
      as tight as a fingernail
opens over the lunch-time pasta

and above the Twin Towers the smoke
      of human flesh appals,
poor Shelley is roasted now, his blue
      eyes like broken glass,
and all the charred smoke rises and rises

in the greasy air, and so poorest Mary
      is glad at this cremation,
or they'd play croquet with his bones,
      use his skull as an ashtray,
those capitalists without mercy,

who mean to turn my continent
      into their Disneyland,
and bomb my people wanting peace,
      from the safety of their
electronic fortresses and deep vaults,

who only want freedom to do the same,
      and Mary weeps for her Shelley
who knew the wind only is free or whatever –
      bloweth where it listeth
he said, with the tang of his corpuscles:

the wind, he offered her, and his breath
      which the brave ribs held
for Shelley is dead, his chest open,
      and the casket for his heart
set to close on its bloody trophy.

With vomit the bay is polluted,
     those bad mad cows
sick on their own entrails
     rolled in relish at McDonald's
and sold for the human jaw to lick up

and vomit forth in the capitalist's lap.
     His board is a cow vulva,
an udder he squeezes for sauce,
     nor are the parts related
any longer as he shakes the Pentagon

like grit in his soup, for Mary
     is without appetite
with her darling husband turned fish,
     the forelock curled about
his sensitive ear like a comma.

And we'll order a continent to eat
     at our table, they say,
and Mickey Mouse and Donald Duck
     will at last reproduce
at my gorgeous last bay of all

at the Cape, where the south-easter blows
     to no effect whatsoever
over Crossroads and Ceres and Karoo,
     driving the burning land
to cinders like poor Shelley's body,

while for Mary the wind in its treachery
     turned over that frail sailing-
craft that is a husband's journey
     and pleasure, never to presume
himself a master of a fate his own

as the American Airlines flight is announced
    to set off to its destination
of the Twin Towers where banquet
    the capitalist and his crew –
those who are forever without mercy.

II

At the Shelley Open-air Cinema
    these heartfelt images flicker:
like a ghost tyranny is come again,
    the New Empire is silver
and gold for the G8 in deadly Genoa

and the poor, the poorest of the poor, swarm
    once more under the pediment
of new Augustus, Napoleon on high,
    those containers of Pakistanis
dying for smuggled air and water, dumped

and projected now in Shelley Cinema
    for every English poet drowned
a hundred Moroccans are washed up,
    where in hired, private deckchairs
the rich tan openly in blue Italy,

where from Senegal and Somalia invade
    the fresh slaves in parkas and trainers
who salaam their other strict God
    and learn to fly where only pilots
need to go, worshipping their airy privilege

here in blue Italy, so like my home:
    where the poorest of the poor
help our ruler have his own airstrip built
    for fear that they fly him
adrift into his own palace in Pretoria.

These are the new Ariel men: Bush,
     Blair, Mbeki – bland politicos,
who fly privately at night, undetected.
     None of them are people's poets
as Shelley intended. Poets are kept in gaol.

And Mary who waits weeping, her weeds
     unchanged, eyes hollow with grief,
stutters at the raging panorama of wave
     and cloud and dread thunderbolt
and says on the subtitle: *A storm, a storm!*

Cut to Mary with casket, his Protestant remains.
     Was he the last to protest in rage
in a great tradition? Keats is gone too,
     and Byron, while Coleridge
and Wordsworth blather on and on:

is there no one left to let shine
     those free words of faith,
such insult and rage, making laws
     ahead of them all: be free,
speak plain, associate, break down?

Pull from the sky like King Kong
     the misguided planes, the falling
bodies-to-be in duffels and tracksuits,
     the bursting diners and bombers,
World Trade in bodies visible at last.

And Mary pushes her shaking hand
     down her gaberdine thigh
where dear Shelley went, entered,
     and as she shakes, she cries out,
O wretched one, restless, drowned at last!

Drowned, nibbled by fishes, a boat of bones,
    a stench in the nostrils with lime,
three bodies on the strand, with oil
    and wine, committed Homeric style,
warriors for peace, obey the sanitary law.

And on the Riviera, the rich and the splendid
    in private deckchairs sniff
that cannibal odour of charred meat,
    order an aperitif earlier,
before sauna and lunch, cashing their chips.

In Shelley Cinema the viewers are placid,
    their dream-state made clear,
as Mary leans for the casket and kisses
    the velvet lining, his hank
of hair and stares bleakly forth…

So that is her life is all, is all,
    a careless rebel who underrated
the wrath of the universe, power of gods,
    a mere mortal meatiness
swallowed in flame and now aery spirit…

this romantic token and only the words:
    bomb, liberate, crush, whelm!
Do not persist without change, draw!
    Die for your cause, do not rest,
peace comes after the plunge, adore!

And as the Twin Towers now implode
    for the nth time as on CNN,
and the rest of the world more or less stops
    as well, warmed and bare,
so the end-credits roll in Shelley Cinema:

featuring the one and only Percy Bysshe Shelley
     and Mary Godwin his loving wife
with bit players Osama bin Ladin
     and Yasser Arafat and too fast
to read now: all who fear flying,

a scroll of seven thousand New York dead
     and all the list of the camps
and gulags swarm over the screen,
     from the millions to billions
of human names up on the screen at last,

every single person and their voices
     crying like Mary, oh God, oh God,
in her desolation, and the soundtrack
     swells with a chorus of outrage
for all those harmed, who were innocent,

and tyranny is abroad yet again, once more,
     and the masque of the conqueror
copyrights death in its global studio,
     only it may live, announcing
THE END, THE END. And it's over.

And Mary shuffles off her metal chair
     in the balmy night, passes a hand
over her face, older now, wiser,
     and raises her eyes to the stars
and Milky Way – still there, not gone yet,

and crushes the stub of her ticket,
     deposits it in the tidy bin,
walks still with some grace for her lodging,
     all these modern inventions,
she's impressed, a bit technophobe.

Shelley, she said, it's all very well,
     stay-sails and ballast and rope,
at the tiller you read Sophocles, not the charts,
     you say you are blessed,
blessed as always but learn to swim.

You must take the most elementary defence,
     you defend poetry that carries you –
abaft like that golden pinioned
     stupid quacking gull –
but why don't you defend your own life?

And now from the Twin Towers, is it
     a trick of the camera? –
those tumbling bodies have learnt to fly,
     take off under wingspreads,
insects all over the smoke of New York City

and Arnold Schwarzenegger shoves them off,
     like gnats in a hazy dream:
shoo (with accent), I must zave you,
     but how may I do my mission
if you have all zaved yourzelves?

On the shore at Lerici, now an attraction
     in the Gulf of Poets, Mary Shelley
finds no rest as the wavelets touch
     her bare feet on the sand,
it is quiet at last, no soundtrack, no doom,

finds no rest and no longer believes in
     the thought of any redemption,
it's only hatred and powder, the hopelessness
     of aging without mercy
and cash, derelict as the driftwood.

Depressed again, she has no wild words
     of defiance against disgrace;
for they flew when they should not fly,
     sailed when they couldn't swim,
drew water, dragged and overturned.

He was bringing the groceries home on a
     domestic run, dear curly-hair,
when the waves inverted him, down,
     and her lungs fill as his did
with salty tears, and she has to blow nose.

They're used to her, the crowd from the cinema,
     standing gaunt on the promenade,
understand the world's a great showpiece
     with special effects and God
knows what marvels. But for her it's real.

When out of the slop dead Shelley comes
     like a ghost as he was wont,
a faint moony mouth, a cowl,
     hovering over the depths
on poisoned waters and plastic bags,

over the dead Mediterranean which connects
     to the dead Atlantic and Indian
and the whole wide garbage-strewn Pacific
     and all the foul brown planet
and he opens his mouth, as was his habit:

Beloved, he says… that you must never doubt:
     my love for thee, real love…
that was the romantic way and all else,
     all else, was supposed to
follow, in a golden necklet without end,

as you know. We did intervene,
    threw the weight of the world
away from oppression and spleen, made
    over that prison and broke that
chain, we made laws anew for sweet people, yes…

But his gauzy, ghostly visage shrivels
    before her, into ash,
into dust, and she treads it down
    once and for all in the tar,
blinks and says, That's really enough now.

And her widow's jaw chews on a lump
    of mashed cow vulva,
for she has to keep up her strength,
    edit the fragments and even the follies,
ruefully she swallows down McDonald's

as the near-dead tumble from the Twin Towers
    over New York and the JSE closes,
and a big milkcow comes to nuzzle beside her,
    pokes her mad head
in the manger and farts pure methane…

So this is the end of history and its belief,
    The Word has gone too,
the bottom fallen out and no escape exit
    in case of fire or foreigners,
just fry there, on a griddle of flame.

And Mary strokes the stupid, daft bovine,
    which says, No cud, no moo, no
baby Jesus, I'd better eat my own
    ground-up kin, squirt
poison milk across the darkening universe…

when Mary the correct one calls the bull,
    symbol of what else but regeneration,
allows him to mount his mate, when from
    his iron pizzle eject
uranium and plutonium in hot spurts…

and now even Mary's gone mad and eaten up,
    too rotting even to curse,
and she just subsides and only can think,
of all things, of the Blue Danube

which encloses her fruit

and waltzes on –

(After visiting Lerici near La Spezia
    on 11 September 2001
and my dear Bellagio thereafter, finished
    in Johannesburg my home):

so I take your apple, polish it on my shirt,
bite.

* * *

64 Short Poems

Only Simple Poems for 1993

They're wanted by *The S. A. Review of Books:*
in other words, back in your box, boy,
get back in your box, back in your box,
boy, get back in, do get back in your box. Boy.

On Some South African Poets

About reviewers they complain in long retorts:
I'm there with you, I also undergo 'em;
Misread, misunderstood, however much they hate bad sports
I sympathise, but where's the bloody poem?

S. A. History

Prematurely he ejaculates at Slagtersnek,
But still he helps himself, hand as woman;
The syllabus to matric is one Great Trek,
The promised gland erect, his second cominq.

Hillbrow Streetcorner

"Hy kan my slaan, hy kan my skop,
Ek's van die plaas af, hy's die baas;
Maar ek sal nie doodgaan, domkop,
Ons gaan almal dood... hy kan raas."

Eating Mulberries with Matthew

Picking the fruit from the tree the two wise queens
Know better 'n to belong to Auden's Homintern,
Spit or swallow, sifting the ripe from the has-beens,
New birthmarks on their lips, they live-'n-learn.

The Anthropologist

Before the Trinity of bow-wows grabbed his soul to dirty hell,
Frazer used his golden bough to beat down all blacks,
In the borderlands where totems spent and swell,
Transfixion of the nons, disregarding facts.

Another

Malinowski also poled the mangrove swamps of sex,
From the negro-trades view and the plantation,
Listed prenuptial intercourses and post,
Anthropologised voyeurs without explanation.

Yet More

Even passive observation participates, intrudes,
Turning hands-on turn and turn about to footage,
Those ethnographic D. C.s, celebrated prudes,
Reduced to tomes the lesser races for their New Age.

Concluding

After all I find that psychologist, Octave Mannoni,
Who measured Prospero's and Robinson's white sword
Against Caliban's and Friday's cut goneys,
In the rebel colonies, taught only to fetishise the Lord.

Vandals

Holtby and Gandhi've had their libraries burnt
By pangamen and raging strugglistas,
No RDP priorities fixing ceilings, shelves,
And cataloguing peace and private vistas.

How to Boil an Egg

The water must boil; lower egg in spoon,
Invert the timer… clean the cup, young man,
When the sands are through, remove, tap, consume.
Now to lay an egg's harder; only chickens can.

How d'you Like your Eggs, Sa?

Two to order: poached sun-up to flavour,
soft, fried or hard to please,
scrambled on toast or as a favour
chef'll insert an omelette with cheese.

Easter Bunnies

Only an Easter Bunny could lay a chocolate egg,
The passover roll-over bucktooth rabbiting on,
The tribal scar, the risen fur and quivering leg,
Thump – dark sweetness – and marshmallow come.

Edward Lear Draws the *Procavia capensis* (1832)

Sticky-pawed basker from the Cape called hyrax
Or dassie; no eagles patrol above the grey London Zoo.
But worse, dark-eyed regards me sketch her pelt in parallax,
Her whiskers mildly luminous, having nothing else to do…

The Former Regime

They were the country's Covenanters, the unelected
Elect, living opaquely above their Laws,
Selected millions for Poverty, Dispossession, Neglect –
That trinity the Brothers worshipped behind closed doors.

An Ethical Problem

Dr Banda's helicoptered back to Garden City,
The question's purely ethical and all:
For 600 victims do they clear his brain without pity,
Or for each shove a finger through his eyeball?

Tribute

Desegregate the railways, states the official communiqué,
Tactfully heroising that old partner in unity,
After he'd divided them of course previously…
And the biggest landholder in Africa (that no one'll say).

Old Comrade

Afraid of bang bang from those you fed by hand,
Move on, comrade, dead they'll you adore;
Rigored your fist still clasps the land,
The young and their children's children want more.

Pik Botha at Joe Slovo's Funeral

Last of the world's Commies, Sunset Joseph, with First
At last; snugger than doxa, surer than indemnity;
Housed with King Arthur in Avalon; versed
In no sacred psalms; only Joe slogans and hypocrisy.

Thieves of the Festive Season

This is their motive: greedy and left-out,
So they filch, lift, swipe, burgle, break-in;
And this is the choice as victims retaliate:
Feed them finely or lose them a limb.

Christmas Swim, 1995

Thanks to the drought the water-level lowers,
Rescuing the laden, chlorinating bee.
Listening for the convergence of lawnmowers,
I take my festive exercise with ease.

New Year's Eve, 1996

My loving family forgets to phone, blah blah...
I survey the past alone... well, I'm alive;
My job: side-drummer who assaults the orchestra,
Against all the rules, in Nielsen's Five.

Phone Repair

When your line is down, I fix the buzz,
I fix the hum, manipulate this lever;
Tap your wire, adjust your joint; doer does;
Now ready to connect, speak into the receiver.

Olive Schreiner Appears in *Playgirl*

Sweet Jesus, hoary men with upstanding cocks
(Surely a trick of the light, a prosthetic device),
Poked at my pleas for freedom; Boks in sweaty socks,
Arise, cover your Long Toms, learn to etherialise.

Reflex Action

Whether it's the late Ken Saro-Wiwa or my cat,
At the moment of death, they can't help it,
Their tongues. They have the whole world to point them at.
Receive that kiss, jaw-tie, stroke, bury it.

On a Nigerian Theory Held in Tel Aviv

The circumscription of your orature,
My phonic lab, my reader response…
The slave route, the bulge impure,
This warm rain, this African song and dance.

Nametags

A conference of gathered papers and parts,
What's the trick of, the trap of our master sex?:
Hisham, Hillel exploded in *The Jerusalem Post*.
Who are you then? Peace (our onomastics).

Fundamental Matters

Newton saw a fruit fall. Downward.
Heading south. He named it gravity.
Apple. A crisp-cheeked and brown word,
Bitten and gulped. Like knowledge. Like depravity.

Some New Planet

This time Venus swims into my silver ken:
Down to earth, like bathmat footprints, between us.
The dusty spores, shrunken space, old women, other men;
Tangled, telescoped. At least one growing, springy phallus.

The Romance of it All

She takes off her hair – I remove
My teeth; she loosens her stay –
I tighten my girth; she reproves
My fumble – I delay, delay.

Two New Positions Taken

When the man holds her back to delay,
That's known as the *waiting* or *wagkamer*;
When the man sings "I'll Do It My Way"
As his mistress descends, that's *Kama Sinatra*.

Something to Hold on to

Where have we met before? Why? When?
I know so well you were once above/beneath/behind me;
The intimate spot that starts most men.
We've loved and will again: remind me.

One Kugel to Another

"It's not what's between your ears but between your legs
That counts; with men they're all the same, young or old;
If he gives it to you, eat on a hotdog and soft-boiled eggs:
Take whatever comes and swallow. You'll be rewarded sevenfold."

Revolutionary Murders

This cocktail with a toothpick in the olive of his head,
Twenty million revolutionary murders done –
Over-the-top Joe the Surrealist – all bloody dead;
Trotsky brings the score to Tequila plus One.

Headcount

Moscow's old archives don't balance:
The final score was twenty-one million
Or two, without right of correspondence,
Figures in columns, released from oblivion.

Dearly Beloved

Guess who's coming back and platsak,
Watch your wallets and cards and purses,
To stand trial: Allan Boesak, Allan Boesak,
Dipped his fingers in the font, switched mercies.

Dream Programme

Caught me unconscious, without my shirt and vest,
Writing automatic beyond the bourgeoisie,
Knowing the unknown, making the latest manifest,
Thus stripped hopeless, I wait and can only see.

Dogs Greet their Bob

So there are none in his kingdom of sodomites come;
We dogs'll sniff if his knob is big, bigger, bigot;
Held by gum, inside the twat or bum –
Reeks of cervix or sphincter, sexy or shithot?

The Deputy-Minister

To recover the Arts from their historic burden,
This she ministers, the nation's matriarch:
Eliminate first all dykes and gays as unAfrican,
And if any worker's left, let 'em strike matches in the dark.

A Debate

"Go to the bush-toilets to do your business there,"
Said Adelaide M. P. to the Minister of Lands,
Instead of stalling with the House where rules are fair –
And arses wiped on white paper, not bare hands.

Requiem for a Shark

Christ is risen, but you are not;
Yet you eat flesh as they do, theophages.
Humbly clean and polish. Surely was forgot.
Is there no salt in heaven for the scavenger of ages?

All our Ganymedes Raped

Jove's chosen one, chaste and nearly neuter,
A temperate shy Trojan, the raptor's feast;
By this beak pecked, prong forced up, feathery suitor:
A last glimpse of soil between his blooded feet.

My Trip (1996)

How to hold the centre in my marginalia?
A long trip abroad, I become hysterical.
How in one quatrain to compress the penetralia –
My whole holiday in all of wide America?

Mustang Statue outside the TX Museum

As good as his horse only was Man in Texas,
Wild meat, unbridled foalers and plunging hooves;
Now the howdy rough riders of the urban nexus
Go for Chevvie fenders and horns and rollback roofs.

This is What we're Talking about

The brown-and-white squirrel, twenty fleet needles
Up a tree grip air, designed as must be;
Out of his element pretends, cocky and heedless:
On level glass a stain like spilt coffee.

I Remember West Coast Religion

To San Francisco I went to see the Cockettes
Performing on a cliffside, naked and stoned:
Double-stoned, cut or uncut, homos 'n hets –
Christ in his crib in their ghetto, big-boned.

Charmides, According to Plato

"His full face you praise, held above a tanktop vest,
Cute is his slack lip, hornier and hornier;
But all that you'll forget once you get him undressed,
The rest of him's more gorgeous than all of California."

Wandering Albatross

Only on Inaccessible they breed,
Temperate and dependent, a last handful.
Do I believe their winged seed
Will prosper on this, their last landfall?

Poème Millénaire

To be buried in Père Lachaise
Under chestnuts and closer to heaven,
Is harder than anyone says –
Above the Métro, Paris 97.

The Louvre

Which way to the Mona Lisa?
Beyond the allegory of this world
And all its ills, and about Africa
They were always wrong, the old masters.

The Necessity of Atheism

At last I have read Shelley's blasphemous rigmarole:
The existence or otherwise of that unproven Deity,
Disbelief's no crime for either lord or provo,
And truth for all mankind more opportune. Q. E. D.

Lightning Rods of Heaven

Rubén Darío of Nicaragua proclaims God,
Burdened with all His electrical celestial flashes,
Chooses the poet – waiting inspiration – as his rod:
But I remark such discharge renders only ashes.

Indeed, Kelwyn, Where are the Classics?

Unlike you to praise the failures of the old arrière-garde;
Oops, satire, I figure, being argumentative;
Once their haikus come to plop, lyrics flop and reviews so retard,
I must agree: poetry will need its sole representative.

At the Poetry Launch

About what he cd've, wd've, shd've done
He chunters on, while a baby sighs and screams,
A jumbo overhead ejects a block of multiracial piss,
While the poet ums and oohs about his unfulfilling dreams.

On Antjie Krog's Husband's Member

Admit, ou boet, you're not so wild
As you used to be, as true as the Lord,
So come your guts and be reconciled,
All manly sins forgiven, and limply bored.

White is a Metaphor

Skinner's on air again, doesn't know his parts
Of speech from his dildo; White is a figure of rhetoric:
The epidermal superficies and Call me Baas,
Outer part for inner whole, you stupid prick!

Horning in

Unstoppable instrument, and having pissed,
His penis drips... he must confess;
Knots, nappies, tourniquets, the tanga-twist
Cannot, alas, persuade his tract to retrogress...

L'art Poetique

As Poe said of Longfellow, a very great man
In a small way, so I find Berold taller
And greater and better informed and just more grand
Than any other poet, only smaller.

On Some South African Academics

From theses to faeces they externally examine,
From Plaatje to potty-talk they theoretically strain;
Publish intellectual words on dunnies full of turds and jasmine-
Scented Sanpic. Their pages do absorb, I can't complain.

The Centenary of the Siege of Ladysmith

To the relief of Juana Maria Dolores de Leon,
Redvers Buller with howitzers two, Castor and Pollux,
Dug deep her defensive trench, no love's peon,
No wire-puller he and shot off his shaft and bollocks.

The Riddle of the Sphinx

"What goes on four legs, on two, then on three?"
A man in his ages, of course. Then, "What stinks
Like a lynx, pees like a mare, can riddle-me-ree
And has double breasts?" Could it be sphinx?

Somewhere over the Rimbaud Nation

"Nuance is all," said Verlaine, "for the rest
Is literature." I reign in my parataxis.
My queer has been pitched, you caught me with his pants
Down. So all that's left is prophylaxis.

Elegy on an Ancestor

The curfew tolls the knell of parting day
And leaves the world to darkness and to us,
Tombstone research has become my way,
And so I prepare my silent exodus.

A Last Simple Epigram, 2003

So our police have fallen on deaf years,
I've (h)armed myself as the decade's democrat of wit,
Of ad-hocery made mockery, assaulted my peers:
I'd better cease up, before the fan hits the shit.

* * *

The Leper Band

"I personally don't know anyone who has died of AIDS. I really honestly don't."
    – Thabo Mbeki

Dead already in their isolation,
Untouchable for their contagion,
The lepers gather in smasher and waistcoat
On parade, holding their mellow note:

Onward Christian soldiers marching as to war,
From ward to church, and repeat as before;
The drums they beat till their hands drop,
Tongues twist about when they have to stop.

Once their feet go, they may hobble,
Bones for crutches, ears in trouble:
O Sarie Marais is so ver van my hart,
At the poor cemetery they had to part.

Then their sons on harmonicas insist on more
And the bugler boy's learning to read the score;
From the church to their prison they swarm and go,
Blowing their guts out, fortissimo.

Most were kept from seeing a leper discompose,
Lesions, through to the bridge of the nose;
In their colonies with a shot now cured,
Each Lazarus is raised, a miracle ensured.

Yet their wild stomp persists in the memory…
How the Governor flinched in his gloves and glory,
Taking that tribute he could barely endure:
From such deprivation, a melody so pure.